Phoebe Clappsaddle
Has a
Tumbleweed Christmas

Phoebe Clappsaddle
Has a
Tumbleweed Christmas

By Melanie Chrismer

Illustrated by Virginia Marsh Roeder

PELICAN PUBLISHING COMPANY
Gretna 2004

Thank you, Dad, for making Christmas fun and
teaching me about the Lord Jesus Christ
—M. C.

For all my family and all their support
—V. M. R.

The word "Pelican" and the depiction of a pelican are trademarks
of Pelican Publishing Company, Inc., and are registered
in the U.S. Patent and Trademark Office.

Library of Congress Cataloging-in-Publication Data

Chrismer, Melanie.
  Phoebe Clappsaddle has a Tumbleweed Christmas / by Melanie Chrismer ; illustrated by Virginia
Marsh Roeder.
     p. cm.
  Summary: In the midst of Texas wind and tumbleweed, Phoebe Clappsaddle, acting sheriff, straightens
out a mail mixup and hostesses a Christmas dinner for the Tumbleweed brothers and other neighbors.
  ISBN 1-58980-241-1 (hardcover : alk. paper)
  [1. Cowgirls—Fiction. 2. Christmas—Fiction. 3. Tumbleweeds—Fiction. 4. Texas—Fiction.
  5. Humorous stories.] I. Roeder, Virginia Marsh, ill. II. Title.
PZ7.C4515Ph 2004
[E]—dc22

08·2249
Pelican Pub
(BHW)
C.2004
9108
$ 18·85

2004003455

Printed in Singapore
Published by Pelican Publishing Company, Inc.
1000 Burmaster Street, Gretna, Louisiana 70053

PHOEBE CLAPPSADDLE
HAS A TUMBLEWEED CHRISTMAS

Phoebe Clappsaddle heard the bell and found Festus Boondoggle delivering her mule mail. He was riding Comet, his mule, and faithful Rudolph was nearby.

"M-m-morning, Phoebe," said Festus, but his greeting was drowned out by Phoebe's gleeful shout.

"Yeehaw! I have mule mail!"

Mail didn't come every day in the territory south of Big Spring, west of Marathon, north of Terlingua, and east of El Paso, but it was Christmastime. Phoebe had a parcel!

"Merry Christmas, Festus," Phoebe said sweetly, handing him an invitation to Christmas dinner.

Festus tipped his hat, said "H'yaw, Comet!" and rode off hollering, "The Tumbleweeds have mail, too!"

Phoebe read the parcel's perfect lettering. It was addressed to Eustace, Clifford, and Elmo Tumbleweed. Festus had made a mistake!

Phoebe tied a bandanna around some gingerbread cowboy cookies and saddled Julep. The Tumbleweed brothers were gnarly cowpokes who didn't always do what they should. Folks called them the Tumbleweed Gang. Good or bad, Phoebe knew they deserved their mule mail, and they might have hers.

As Phoebe traveled past the crag, she looked at the
gray sky. Snowy clouds made her tighten her scarf.
Seeing the two-pronged pickle fork in the road, she
knew she was close to Tumbleweed Canyon.

Phoebe spotted Clifford and Elmo arguing up a storm. They didn't even notice her until Dawg gave a friendly welcoming "Ruff."

Clifford let go, and Elmo loosened his lariat. Phoebe was the acting territory sheriff, and they knew it.

"Who sent the sheriff?" grumbled Clifford, rolling a cactus toothpick around his mouth.

"Twern't me," burped Elmo.

"No one," said Phoebe. "I'm delivering your mail." She untied her scarf, revealing the tin star, and asked, "Do y'all need a sheriff?"

"Yep," said Eustace.

"Keep that kettle away, Eustace," warned Clifford. Turning to Phoebe, he said, "OK, *Sheriff* Clappsaddle, the problem is someone around here is stealing."

The three brothers squinted at each other.

"Too bad no one stole Eustace's chili," added Elmo, holding his nose.

"Eustace is no use to us as a cook," agreed Clifford. "Ever since he's been reading cookbooks, he's been poisoning us."

The boys started fighting again, so Phoebe sidestepped and grabbed Elmo's piggy rope. In a flash, Clifford was hogtied, Eustace was ear-nabbed, and Elmo was lassoed to the porch. She convinced them to sit quietly.

"Everything takes practice," said Phoebe, opening her bandanna, "even cooking. Come for Christmas, and I'll teach Eustace some sure-fire recipes."

Looking around, she asked, "So what's missing?"

"My hat, Elmo's shirt, and Eustace's bandanna," Clifford mumbled, spitting crumbs.

"We thought Dawg took 'em," said Elmo, licking his fingers. "But that critter's too fat and just stays under the porch."

"Yep. Eats everything," Eustace bragged.

"Hmm," said Phoebe. Then Phoebe pulled out the parcel. "Festus delivered this to me," she said. "And I believe you have my mule mail."

"Go check the box, Elmo," ordered Clifford.

"More reading!" groaned Elmo, bringing a letter.
"This one's from Miz Hornswaggle," said Eustace,
reading the parcel front.

Elmo handed Phoebe the letter, and sure enough,
it was addressed to Miss Phoebe Clappsaddle.

"Hoo-wee! Homework?" complained Clifford.

"One, two, um—twenty-eight pages!" Elmo exclaimed. He loved counting, now that he knew his numbers.

"Yep," added Eustace. "A book! Me first!"

"Dee-lightful," said Phoebe. "Miss Hornswaggle sent y'all a Christmas poem and me a beautiful card."

"Wouldn't that curdle your gizzard?" grumbled Clifford. "Our teacher sent us reading when we're on holiday break."

Eustace, the best reader of the three, only had trouble reading "S'ain't Nickel-less." A blast of wind told Phoebe it was time to go.

"Behave, Tumbleweeds," she said. "And come to Christmas dinner."

Hearing "dinner," they all said, "We'll be there!"

The wind blew harder. A big storm was coming, and Phoebe knew she had to hurry. "Ride like the wind, Julep," Phoebe said. She held her hat with one hand and Julep's reins with the other. Both ladylike pinkies were up.

Phoebe put Julep in the barn and hoped the cover over that hole in the barn roof would hold.

Peeking out the window, Phoebe remembered the shepherds and their critters on the first Christmas night. She smiled and had a peaceful Christmas Eve.

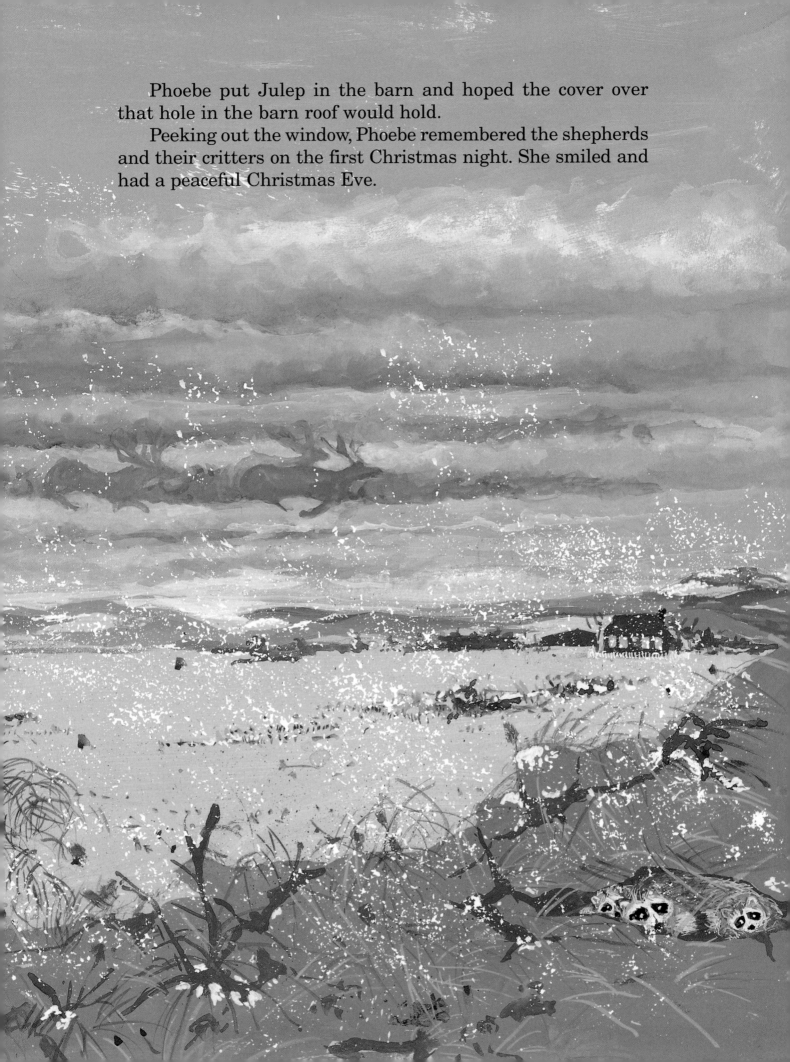

On Christmas morning, Phoebe's house was decorated top to bottom.

Before everyone arrived, she had to check the barn for damage and feed all her critter friends.

Expecting a white Christmas, Phoebe could hardly believe her eyes. She saw tumbleweeds—mounds and mounds of tumbleweeds!

Phoebe waded through tumbleweeds to the barn. On the way back, she heard the first visitors arrive.

"Hello-ho-ho and howdy!" called Festus, walking through the prickly drifts. A sweet, white-haired lady with rosy cheeks was with him.

"The missus and I thought you could use some brown-sugar candy."

Phoebe was thanking him, when hollering came from behind the barn. Festus, his missus, and Phoebe followed the sound. There, in the corral, the Tumbleweed brothers were having fun.

Clifford was throwing tumbleweeds at Elmo. Elmo was making a tumbleweed man. Eustace was making a tumbleweed angel in the dirt.

"Looks like we're having a tumbleweed Christmas," said Phoebe.

When they spotted the others, the boys jumped up and said, "We brought presents!" There was a barbed wire wreath, a rattlesnake rattle garland, and Eustace's cooking pot.

Clifford added, "And, look! S'ain't Nickel-less came!"
"We got puppy presents!" said Elmo.
"Yep!" exclaimed Eustace.
Dawg beamed with pride at her brood. Rudolph looked
proud too. Festus gave him a sideways glance.

"Those pups look like somebody I know," he said, giving Rudolph a pat.

"Let's eat," Phoebe said.

She looked in Eustace's pot and thanked him. He had tried to make molasses cookies. Now she could fix the barn roof. They would make perfect shingles.

Later, they all went back outside, piled up tumbleweeds into a Christmas-tree shape, and decorated it. Elmo counted how many times he was able to wrap the rattle garland. Mrs. Boondoggle tied ribbons here and there, and Phoebe placed her sheriff's badge at the top.

"Merry Christmas, y'all," said Phoebe.

And merry it was, in the territory south of Big Spring,
west of Marathon, north of Terlingua, and east of El Paso.